After

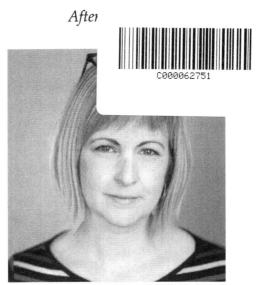

C000062751

Photo by Charles Leek

Rose Condo is a Canadian poet based in Salford, England. With a background in theatre, she has been writing, performing and teaching for over twenty years and was longlisted for the inaugural Jerwood Compton Poetry Fellowship. Rose has won numerous poetry slams and her poetry theatre show, *The Empathy Experiment*, received critical acclaim at the 2019 Edinburgh Fringe and won Best Spoken Word Show at the 2019 Greater Manchester Fringe.

"Rose Condo's name is synonymous with powerful verse, enthralling spoken word theatre, astute dissections of modern life, and superhuman empathy. Hers is work that refuses to accept half-baked assumptions, choosing instead to dig with precision to the roots of the world's ugliness."

— *Geneviève L. Walsh*
spoken word artist

"I have never seen her fail to connect with any audience with her honest, unflinching, charming and deeply human poetry. Global influences have helped shape a strong, grounded and world-aware voice. A generous artist who is a consistent joy to experience on the page and stage."

— *Dominic Berry*
Glastonbury Festival poet-in-residence 2017

"A sensitive and compassionate approach to some of the most difficult and pertinent questions in life. Rose has a unique way of making palatable that which we often struggle to look at. Honest, soulful and full of heart, her skill with words is deft and her message is a reassuring embrace at a time of universal uncertainty."

— *Alex Slater*
poet & writer

"If there were ever a time for kindness and empathy, it's now. Rose Condo's poems are a steadying reminder of compassion, in a world tipped off its axis."

— *Rosie Garland*
poet & novelist

"Great for poets wondering how to superbly stitch together a solo show. Rose Condo is a wonderful, soothing and soulful poet. Her poetry is a friend when the world is a storm."

— *Louise Fazackerley*
poet

"A heart-warming collection, full of humanity and hope."

— *Rosie Fleeshman*
spoken word artist

"This collection is a hearty meal after a long journey. These nourishing poems will comfort, soothe and restore the weary. A steady dignity and strength underpin explorations of belonging, creativity and connection. The idea of these poems finding their way to more people through this collection makes me very happy indeed."

— *Ciarán Hodgers*
poet

February 2023

Carol & Dave

A wee book as a thank you for both the great trip to Madeira and supporting our Acoustic Amnesty event.
May the road rise to you both.
Love,
Serpil & Steven
xxx

ROSE CONDO
After *the* Storm

Flapjack Press
www.flapjackpress.co.uk

Exploring the synergy between performance and the page

Published in 2020 by Flapjack Press
Salford, Gtr Manchester
⊕ flapjackpress.co.uk
f Flapjack Press ✔ FlapjackPress

ISBN 978-1-9161479-5-9

Cover photo by Charles Leek
⊕ charlesleek.com ◎ staggerleek

Illustrated by Jen McDonald
◎ jen.m.cd

Music by Eleonora Rosca
◎ eleonorarosca

"QR Code" is a registered trademark of
Denso Wave Incorporated

FSC

Printed by Imprint Digital
Upton Pyne, Exeter, Devon
⊕ digital.imprint.co.uk

To all who – beyond the aftermath –
Have helped to guide and light my path

Contents

A version of 'You Are Here' previously appeared in *Evidently: The Anthology, Vol. 2* (2015) and in *The London Reader* (Winter 2017).

A version of 'Flash Drive' previously appeared in the *Say Owt Anthology, Vol. 1* (2015).

Foreword

I first met Rose in the last week of the 2014 Edinburgh Fringe, when she came to perform her show, *The Geography of Me*. I had seen a lot of shows by then. I mean A LOT. I'd been at the Fringe for the whole of August with my own show, *The Good Delusion*, and by that point my compassion had worn thin and my cynicism was riding high. I went to Rose's show, mainly because we were in the same venue and I felt obliged, as Venue Captain, to support my fellow artists. After five minutes I had forgotten all about obligation and settled into a wonderful hour of engaging, seemingly simple, but actually profound poetry and storytelling. Even when the end of that show was interrupted by another Fringe performer hammering on the door, Rose carried on, demonstrating a grace under pressure which I now know extends everywhere in her life.

One of our most basic human needs is to be seen and heard. In the transcripts of these three shows, together with their thought-provoking introductions, Rose dives deep into questions that trouble the human condition. Never didactic, she invites the audience on their own voyage of discovery, into how to re-make a life after it has fallen apart, how to nurture yourself, how to discover true intimacy in our over-stimulated world.

We all long for these reminders. In a world that seduces us into believing we need to be turned on, tapped in and super-productive 24/7, Rose reminds us of our humanity, not as a weakness, but a doorway to something larger. A life that we can call our own.

After that first show, Rose gave each audience member a red badge, with the words 'You are here' printed on it. I stuck it on my jacket and when I caught sight of it, found myself sighing with recognition at the truth of those words. I would feel a little more grounded, more present in my body.

Two years later, I put that jacket through the washing machine, along with the badge. It sounds melodramatic to say, but I cried when I saw its faded front, the letters disappearing into the sickly pink the badge had become. I felt bereft, as if I had lost a piece of myself. I confessed this to Rose the next time I saw her, after performing as a guest in her show *How to Starve an Artist*. She dug her hand in her pocket.

"I just happen to have one here."

The new badge went back on my jacket and I have never washed it again.

Tina Sederholm
June 2020

Introduction

It was late Spring 2013. I had just moved to a new town. I had just left an abusive relationship. I was broken and lost.

Pretty intense way to start, eh?

I'm starting here because, well, this is pretty much where my poetry pathways began.

I was in a place of trauma and uncertainty. I knew I needed to rebuild my life and I wasn't quite sure where to begin. I sought healing in all the places I could think of – friends, family, therapy, yoga, meditation … and words.

I was reading a lot. I think I was hoping to find written words that could help me articulate what I had just gone through, and maybe to help me make sense of myself.

Elaine La Joie's book, *The Empath and the Archetypal Drama Triangle*, offered some insight into the drama and trauma I had gone through. I recognised myself in her description of an Empath – someone highly sensitive and deeply attuned to the energies and emotions of others. La Joie's research shows that Empaths frequently end up in abusive relationships, often driven by a need to rescue an abusive partner. This too felt very familiar. La Joie further writes that when an Empath steps away from this kind of situation,

> "…she is free to do whatever she wants in her life. This can be shocking for the Empath. Suddenly she has so much time, space and energy when she stops playing in someone else's Drama. The Empath stepping away from Drama and the Rescuer role is stepping toward personal empowerment and enjoyment of her own creativity."
>
> —La Joie, Elaine. p.33, *The Empath and the Archetypal Drama Triangle: Empath as Archetype Volume One* [CreateSpace Independent Publishing Platform, 2012].

This passage leapt off the page at the time. In all of my healing and recovery, I was also feeling a surge of creativity. I was writing. And writing. And writing. I suddenly had time, space and energy that weren't being drained into my former relationship. Poetry flooded into this new space and offered me creative pathways through the overwhelming things I was dealing with. My writing was giving me clarity and comfort and – somewhat unbelievably – joy.

One afternoon during this time, an image came to mind of the aftermath of a tornado or hurricane. I kept picturing a scene of wreckage and devastation. I realised that I was feeling like I had just gone through a wild and terrifying storm and I was faced with picking up the pieces of my life and putting them back together. I sat down to write what I kept seeing in my mind's eye. So began my poem, 'After the Storm'.

You'll find the poem 'After the Storm' in the first section of this collection. It also felt like the right title for this book because, well, everything you're about to read has come after my storm in late Spring 2013.

Things have definitely changed for the better since then.

I started performing my work at open mic nights. In 2014, a friend invited me to attend a new poetry slam in Manchester called Word War. This brilliant monthly event (along with Evidently, its sister monthly event in Salford) became my gateway into meeting new friends and making new creative and social connections. I won the inaugural Word War Slam Championship that year and started getting booked as a guest for gigs. From 2014-2018, organisers Ella Gainsborough and Kieren King ran these as two of the best spoken word nights in the UK and launched the poetry careers of so many people – including me!

Kieren also asked me out for 'non-poetry related drinks' in early 2017 and – once we both figured out it was actually a date – we've been together ever since.

Alongside all of this, I started attending spoken word shows. Having studied theatre and performance in my home country of Canada, I loved seeing how these shows could weave together poetry, story, performance and narrative. The very first solo spoken word show I saw was Ben Mellor's *Anthropoetry* at the 2013 Edinburgh Fringe Festival. I was awestruck by his clever and captivating exploration of the human body through poetry, story and live music. I bought Ben's book after the show – my first Flapjack Press purchase! Little did I know that later that year I would create my very own first solo spoken word show, *The Geography of Me*.

I have since gone on to write and perform two more shows – *How to Starve an Artist* and *The Empathy Experiment*. What you're now holding is a collection of all three of these shows. It is a wonderfully surreal experience to be sharing these words with you on these pages!

Big gratitude goes out to Flapjack Press for publishing my work, and to Linda Pearce, Ciarán Hodgers and Kieren King for their kind and keen editing eyes.

As you make your way through, you'll notice some participatory elements. My long-time friend and fellow creative soul, Jen McDonald created the illustrations. The QR Codes and the music recordings to which they link were created thanks to my dear friend and wonderful creative collaborator, Eleonora Rosca. These activities are an invitation for you to take part (if you wish) in some of the things I include in my live shows. I do love a bit of audience engagement – for more on that, check out my chapter in the upcoming book, *Spoken Word in the UK* [eds. Lucy English & Jack McGowan].

For now, I hope you enjoy this journey.

Big love,
Rose x
April 2020

The Geography of Me

"A brave, lyrical and vivid evocation of displacement, memory, family and lost love. A bittersweet and inspiring work of art."
— *Susan Burns, Chol Theatre*

This show happened by coincidence in Autumn 2013.

My post-breakup creative writing surge coincided with the start of a new monthly artist development night at the Lawrence Batley Theatre (LBT) in Huddersfield. Chol Theatre (a resident company at the LBT) had been asked to put on a monthly event for artists to test ideas and try out new work. The event was to be called Coffee House Nights and would take place in the LBT's café, Queenie's Coffee Shop.

Chol Director Susan Burns had seen me perform a poem at an event a couple of months earlier. She asked if I'd like to be their first Coffee House Night performer and did I have any new ideas I'd like to try? I said yes and we agreed on a date for the event.

I had no idea what to do.

In preparation, I gathered a stack of poems that I had been writing and spread them out on my living room floor. I thought that if I stared at these words for long enough, and shuffled and rearranged the order, a theme might emerge around which I could build a spoken word show.

It worked!

I felt like my writing explored ideas around journeys – both literally and figuratively. I pieced poems together and wrote a bit of new material. I called the show *The Geography of Me* and I began to rehearse.

I thought about how I could visually represent this theme on stage. I bought a big red suitcase and a rolled-up map of the world. I stuck small red dot stickers on the map for all the places I have visited, and I hung the map from the suitcase handle. LBT Director Victoria Firth suggested I get a round red rug to stand on for the poem 'You Are Here'. A short online order later, I had a red dot rug. This has become one of my favourite performance features ever.

Susan Burns asked if I could include a participatory activity (Chol are big on audience engagement!), so we devised a postcard plan. At the start of the show – as I sang the opening song 'Spin' – I would hand out postcards with a map of the world printed on them. Midway through the show, I would ask the audience to think of a place in the world that is meaningful to them. I would hand out pens and small red dot stickers, asking them to place their dot on that spot on the map and write me a message about that location. I would then take a small red mailbox out of my suitcase and collect the postcards. I would read a few out loud, pin them to my map, and carry on with the show.

Despite massive nerves, my first sharing of *The Geography of Me* went beautifully well. I went on to tour the show to the PBH Free Fringe in Edinburgh, the Winnipeg Fringe Festival in Canada, and many other festivals and events in the UK. Messages on the postcards have been hilarious and heart-wrenching and it has been a joy to share this spoken word journey with people.

On a side note, it is interesting to reflect on how my poem 'True North Confessions', about my experiences of being mistaken as an American, carries a much different meaning now as compared to 2013.

I've also included a version of the postcard activity in this section and I encourage you to have a go!

(During this opening song, I come on stage carrying my big red suitcase. I walk through the audience handing out world map postcards. I take a large world map out of my suitcase, unroll it and hang it from the suitcase handle.)

Spin

Someone once sang
That times are a-changin'
But change isn't easy
When I'm standing still
I'm like the eye of the storm
The world flies around me
I hope that peace comes
And I know that it will

So spin me towards the next curve of this journey
Follow the arc and around I will go
I will face and embrace what lies before me
Thankful for all of the blessings I know

My faith can be weak
When doubt looms so heavy
Having to trust
Through the battles I'm thrown
But my spirit is strong
From the love that surrounds me
Reflections remind me
Of how I have grown

So spin me towards the next curve of this journey
Follow the arc and around I will go
I will face and embrace what lies before me
Thankful for all of the blessings I know

Today it's half empty
Tomorrow half full
The pendulum swings
And I try to hang on
I'm trying to live my life
Moment by moment
Following the feet
That I walk upon

So spin me towards the next curve of this journey
Follow the arc and around I will go
I will face and embrace what lies before me
Thankful for all of the blessings I know

You Are Here

I love to travel. I have done a lot of travelling. A while ago, I did what a lot of travel lovers do. I bought a big map of the world and I put little red dot stickers on all the places I've been to so far. It looks amazing. But the longer I look at it, the more I realise that it doesn't tell enough of the story. The red dots show where I've physically been. But they don't tell anything about the experiences I had or the amazing people I met. I also love to write. I write about my outer journeys in the world and my inner journeys through life. I've pieced together some of that writing, which I'm going to share with you now. A kind of geography of me.

But before I do that, I have a confession to make. I am a huge map nerd. I love to collect maps from the places I've been. I love planning routes on a map. Which is helpful since – rather ironically – I have a terrible sense of direction. My greatest love is for big area maps out in public – like the ones you might find at a train station or in a park. I adore going up to these maps and finding the big red dot on it with the words next to it, 'you are here'. I get genuinely giddy because I can see where I am. I can locate myself, see what's around me, and figure out where to go next. And so, for that reason …

I carry around
A red dot in my bag
So that no matter where I am
I can precisely tag

The place on which I stand
As the very spot
Of exactly where I am
Marked by this red dot

A kind of you are here
For wherever I go

So that no matter where I am
I will always know
You are here

You see there are places that I've been
That don't appear on any map
Some of my travels leave
A geographical gap

Few of these places
Lie within the borders of any nations
My red dot does not apply
To these metaphysical locations

For example I have cruised along denial
I've sat deep in the blues
I've tried to walk miles
In other people's shoes

I've followed in others' footsteps
I've walked along the razor's edge
I've jumped into the deep end
I've gone in way over my head

I've kept my head above water
I've been head and shoulders above
I've worn my heart on my sleeve
I've been head over heels in love

I've been atop cloud nine
I've walked along without a care
I've sometimes crossed the line
I've popped down to the depths of despair

I've spent a few long hours
In the dark nights of my soul
I've gone out on a limb
I've spun out of control

I've had to face the music
I've had to take the upper hand
I've put my foot in my mouth
I've buried my head in the sand

I've been struck down with worry
I've sometimes lost my mind
I've spent days deep in thought
But I always seem to find

My way back to remembering
To stand here on this spot
To let go of my focus
On the places that I'm not

And acknowledge where I am
As the present reappears
So my red dot is my reminder
Hey girl you are here

Queue Forming Nation

One of my favourite ways to travel is by foot. If only I could get everywhere that way. However, since I trek around quite a bit for gigs and workshops, I'm often on the train or on the bus.

I've lived in the UK for several years now and still occasionally notice differences between here and my home country of Canada. For example, in Canada – especially in winter – waiting for the bus means huddling up in and around other people, all of us in thick coats and parkas, possibly subconsciously trying to share body heat. But in the UK, waiting for the bus is very different. Not long ago I was waiting for a bus and I look over and I see ...

This old woman stood drenched in the rain
Wet strands of her grey hair were pasted across her face
She braced herself against the dirty water that splashed
From the careless cars that drove past
She grasped onto the arm of her companion
Another old woman
Who was just as wet
Her face set against the rain
As they stood in the bus stop queue
Along with a dozen others who
Like me were headed into town
The rain poured down

But I was bone dry
One of the lucky five who had arrived first
And stood under the bus stop shelter
At the front of the queue

The bus was due
I looked at the time

And then looked over at the line
That extended out beyond the shelter
And into the rain
But acknowledged the order and time
That each person had arrived at this stop
It was a systematic organization of rain-soaked bodies
Any disruption to this queue would have been unspeakably naughty
Each drenched person in line adhered to the unspoken queue rule
That thou shalt not jump the bus stop queue or else you
Shall face a deluge of dirty looks and an unbearable torrent of tuts

And yet I looked around and noticed
There was more than enough room under the shelter
For everyone who was waiting
This unspoken rule
I thought
Could use some debating

What if
I thought
I shouted down the queue
Hello look here all of you
There is plenty of room under here
Where it's dry
Break free from the queue
Come along
Don't be shy
You
Yes you
All of you
Step up
There is plenty of room under here to bunch up
Standing here where it's dry and out of the rain

Makes so much more sense and is a far more sane
Way to deal with the situation
Of the incessant precipitation
In this queue-forming nation

And people would look up
Shaken out of their queue trance
And glance at each other with glints of hope in their eyes
They would step forward
Ignoring the order of the queue
Transforming from a line into a group
All huddled up and dry standing together
Happy and cheery under the bus stop shelter

Cars would drive by
And drivers would double-take and think
   What the hell has happened to that queue
   That group of people waiting for the bus
   Looks so happy and cheery
The drivers would envy us

We would all be so happy to be out of the rain
We would chat about all sorts
What we'd planned for our days
And the two old women who had inspired my call to action
Would start clapping
Applauding this revolutionary happening
They would tell their friends
And word would spread fast
And news of this one simple noble act
Would ripple across the land
And launch a tide of change
No more standing in the rain
While waiting for the bus

Just because of silly queue rules
It's really too foolish
To follow rules that don't make sense
The entire country would stop such nonsense
Everyone
Everywhere
Would maximise the use of the bus shelter space
And maybe
Just maybe
Engage with each other
Face to face

I envisioned a queue revolution taking over the land
But then the guy in front of me extended his hand
To beckon the oncoming bus
To stop for all of us
I quickly fished into my pocket
For my bus fare
And there in that moment
My revolutionary ideas were abandoned
And I boarded the bus in an orderly fashion

Flash Drive

My love of travelling has meant that I have lived in quite a few different places. Moving around that much means that I have gotten pretty good at whittling down my worldly possessions. Except, unfortunately, for books.

I love books. I love the way they smell, the way they feel in my hands. I once tried reading an e-book and just missed turning pages too much. So, having a minimal number of books is hard for me. Even harder than that is minimising the number of travel journals I have. Writing through my experiences helps me to make sense of the world ... and I have amassed dozens of travel journals. The upside is that I have a detailed record of my journeys. The downside is that the journals take up space. At one point I thought I'd try using a USB stick for my writing. I would carry it around with me and if an idea popped to mind, I'd find a computer, type it up and save. It seemed a much more practical and transportable way of storing my writing. And it worked for a while. However ...

I was working on my laptop not that long ago
And I needed to check how much space I had left
On my three-year-old 8-gigabyte
Carry it with me day and night
USB flash drive

I popped it in the slot
Opened 'My Computer'
Clicked on the external drive icon
And waited for my mile-long list
Of saved files to appear
And after a moment I discovered
To my surprise and despair
That nothing was there
It was empty

The contents had been
Erased or wiped clean somehow
There was not a file to be found
I stifled the sound of panic rising in my throat
No biggie
I tried to assure myself
I'm usually quite stealth
About backing up my work someplace else
And anyway really
What could it have held
Other than some documents and files
And a few old CVs
Nothing that couldn't be retrieved
From my trusty old filing system
She says pointing to her head

Only later did the dread slowly start to sink in
When one day on a whim I wanted to
Locate a certain file and couldn't
I spent a long while searching through
All of my technical storage devices
Even my empty flash drive
I checked it not once but twice
I went through them all
And what I wanted was gone
Even now I can't recall
Exactly what the missing file contained
Except to say
That it was something I had written
The start of a poem perhaps
Or maybe it was the opening of a short story
Whose brilliance
If I had finished it
Would have brought me fame and glory
And now it was gone

And it dawned on me
Like one of those moments
Where you think you can see
A shred of absolute truth about our lives
That this now empty 8-gigabyte flash drive
Was simply an indication
Of our temporary situation
Translation
Nothing is permanent

But where
I wondered
Could I store my written work
So I could 100% ensure
That it would be around
At least as long as I'm alive
Surely there's an alternative to a flash drive
Back to basics
I thought
And do what has been done for ages
I could write my words on paper
But I might lose the pages
What if
I thought
I carved my words onto the trunk of a large old tree?
That should guarantee they'll be around
At least until the tree gets chopped down

For me you see
It's more than just the act of writing
Otherwise I would do nothing but sit by the seaside all day
Writing my words in the sand
And watching them over and over get washed away
And it's more than just sharing my words with others far and wide

Otherwise I would go old school
And write my words by plane in the sky

I could
I thought
Engrave my words onto a sheet of steel
Which I could then affix
Onto a house of bricks built on solid ground
That should ensure my words will hang on
But after a while I'll be long gone

Why, I wondered, is it so important to me to have
A rock-solid record of my efforts in writing
In truth I realise I must borrow the words of another
A champion writer called Djanet Sears
To try to explain my hopes and fears
About giving my writing some permanence
For her
She says
For so many reasons
It's about writing yourself into existence
And saying I was here

I am here
And while I'm around
I'll use my words in the moment
In my present
To be loud and strong and articulate and brave
But tonight when I go home
I'll probably type up this poem
And I'll be sure to hit
File
Save

True North Confession

People often ask where I'm from. I've been told I sound Irish. I was once asked if I'm from Newcastle. Despite having lived in the UK for many years, I still have a strong Canadian accent. When people find out I'm Canadian, the conversations usually go like this: they ask which part of Canada I'm from. I find this hilarious because, with the greatest respect, most folks know of Toronto in the east and Vancouver in the west. They stare at me blankly when I say I'm from Winnipeg in the middle of the prairies. Then – almost without fail – people ask me, 'why are you here?'. My answer is too large to unpack in a casual exchange, so I say that I came here to travel and work and study, and now I live here. Then people always tell me about every person they've ever known that has been to Canada, saying how beautiful it is and how they'd like to visit one day. These conversations are usually full of kindness and curiosity ... but they are always the same!

In truth, however, the question I'm most often asked is if I'm American. It sometimes gets under my skin. I imagine what it would be like to try and confront the big shiny neighbour to the south of Canada. What would I say? Or sing?

> *Oh say can you see*
> *The true north strong and free*
> *We're your neighbour next door*
> *And we're gallantly dealing*

With your broad stripes and bright stars
Leaving oil-thirsty
Natural-resource-hungry scars
All over our sparsely populated landscape
You are omnipotent and full of bravado
You eclipse our nation and leave us in shadow

You are at the centre of the continent we share
Evidence of your influence is everywhere
You leave me keeping quiet in foreign lands
Reluctant to stand out
Because when I open my mouth and speak
Heads spin and eyes snap wide
And I face the inevitable question
The perpetuating assumption
About my country of origin

So are you from America then?

No
I say
Actually I'm Canadian
And if I had a loonie or a nickel or a dime
For every time I get the response

> *Oh Canada*
> *It's pretty much the same*
> *As America isn't it?*

Well hell I'd be rich

We are not the fifty-first state
We are still a relatively different nation
The reality of the situation is that
You are the handsomely dashing
Neon flashing point of comparison
You created and innovated and own
So much of what the world sees
You set the global tone
And it often seems
We're left doing our best impression

Like a kid sister playing dress up
Doing our best to measure up
Trying to our best to come up
With an answer to the question

> *Tell me*
> *What is an example of something uniquely Canadian?*

Well
I stammer as I rack my brain
Grasping for some specific spot on which to stake my claim
Until I realise that's not exactly how we play this game

I mean you are omnipotent and full of bravado
And you eclipse our nation and leave us in shadow
But maybe that's not so bad
Considering the track record we've had
Of abuse of cultures and tribes and bands
Of ongoing theft of indigenous lands
Of our own partial responsibility
For being resource-hungry and oil-thirsty
Of our own huge divide
Between the haves and have nots
So we've got a reputation
For being generally friendlier
My homeland is not utopia
Despite how we get spun in the media

No matter how high I stand
On my soapbox to say
We are not the U S of A
We are still a relatively different nation
The reality of the situation is that
Every day our so-called leaders
March ever further to the right

And every night they cosy up tight
Under the blanket of your star-spangled banner

So then
The manner in which I try to identify
What it means to be Canadian
Will it always be in comparison to you?
The red, white and true beauty
Of the flag that bears the maple leaf
Is a testament to my belief
That we are not a nation built on
World-dominating slogans and golden arches
Our nation is the sum of our multi-cultural parts
We are a melting pot of languages and histories
Traditions and creeds
Simmering with insight and compassion and creativity
And perhaps we will never bear a singular
Loud and proud national identity
But the truth of our spirit and our geography is that

We will always be the true north strong and free

I have another confession to make. I love to receive mail. I love that someone somewhere in the world has thought of me, put pen to paper, written out my address, stuck on a stamp, sent it off to me, and when I receive it I hold in my hands a tangible connection to that person.

With a live audience, I start the show by handing out world map postcards. And then at this point in the show, I hand out little red sticky dots and ask people to put their red dot somewhere on the map that is meaningful to them.

On the back of the postcard, I ask audience members to write me a message about why that place is meaningful. Then I go through the audience holding a red post-box for people to mail their postcard to me instantly – no stamps required. And then I read a few of the messages out.

Since you are reading this in a book, I've included a drawing of the postcard on the next page. If you fancy giving this a go, grab a red pen and draw a dot on a spot on the map that is meaningful to you. Below you'll see a space where you can write a message.

Once you've done that, you can 'post' the message to me on social media (@prairiepetal) and use the hashtag #TheGeographyOfMe.

I look forward to reading your message!

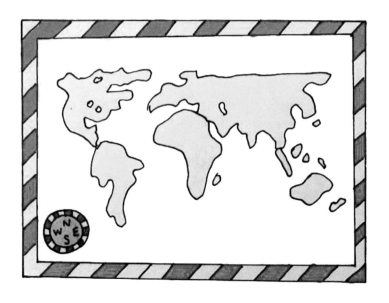

Time Management

I like to be on the go. I like to have a lot of things on the go. Therefore, I'm always pretty conscious of time. In fact, you might say that ...

I am a master craftsperson of time management
I carve time
Shape time
Make time
And find time
I try to keep an eye
On the clock at all times
So that I never
Ever run out of time

I match each task in my day
To an amount of minutes
I say this will take twenty minutes
That should take no more than half an hour
I love the feeling of power
That comes with the control I have over my time
Because I only have a limited amount
We all only have a limited amount
I've no time to break to breathe
Because if I do inevitably
My mind wanders outside of the schedule
I have carefully defined
And I find
I long for the next time
I get to see your face
And can be in the same place
As you

I long for the time when we can
Forget about our limited minutes and days
And lay together for hours on end
And not worry about how we spend
Our time together in the same place

Who has time for these thoughts
Quick
Pick up the pace
Make a list of my to-dos today
And may I please get everything done
I work
I thrive
I run
On keeping control
Over every last minute
Of every last moment
I feel the need
The need to please
Fill each hour up and make the time go by
So that I don't miss you too much

And yet

And yet

I miss you so much
You are with me all of the time
In my thoughts my heart my mind
No matter how many tasks I craft
No matter how much I wish the days would pass faster
No matter how many minutes I master
Hardly a moment goes by
That I don't see you in my mind's eye

And I can't wait for the next time
That I get to see your face
And get to share your space
And can finally
Indefinitely
Be in the same place
As you

She Sleeps

Being far away from people that we love is hard. Being in a place where we're not very happy is hard. We all have our different ways of dealing with this. As you can probably tell from the previous poem, I tend to keep myself really busy. And sometimes there are people in my life who travel so far inward to avoid hard situations, that it can be difficult to stand on the outside watching. It can be hard to see them retreat into darkness and depression, and not know how to reach out and help.

She sleeps
A respite in the night
A breath of peace in between fitful waking

It's taking its toll
This hold
That the darkness has on her

Her friends they say

> *Just take each day*
> *One step at a time*

She tries
But her friends don't realise
That the size of each step forward through
Each and every single moment of
Each and every single day
Is sometimes too much to even contemplate
And so instead
She sleeps
She keeps the darkness flowing
She knows the signs

The red flags that rise
On the ships that pass through her dark nights

She knows this is not just a mood or funk or phase
And on the days when she can't stop crying
She buys into the lies spun by the dark demons in her mind
Like a bad track playing over and over again
She is a sad song stuck on repeat

She reads the books
She watched the experts
Speaking on YouTube
Saying how

> *You Too Can Change Your Life*
> *In Six Easy Steps*

She knows of the tricks
But somehow they still don't fix
The broken-down gate
That can't quite seem to keep the darkness
From finding a way to seep in

And so she binds herself in blankets
Trying to contain
The familiar resistance to change
She shields her eyes
Burrows deep
And she sleeps

After the Storm

I have another confession to make. I am a hardcore list-maker. I love making lists. I love the way lists help me bring some order to what lies ahead. Making a list helps me to feel more prepared for the next part of my journey – whether that journey takes me to the grocery store, or whether that journey takes me across an ocean to live in a new country. When I moved to the UK in 2011, I had made many lists and thought I was prepared for what was to come. However, my journey took an unexpected turn and I found myself on a really rocky road. I was suddenly on a very stormy road. Incidentally, storms are one thing I really miss about living in the Canadian prairies. There is something really powerful about being in the massive expanse of sky and land through thunder and lightning ...

When I was a kid I remember you could see them coming
Steel grey clouds would darken the distant horizon
And drift forward to fill the giant prairie sky
It felt like I could smell the oncoming downpour

Electricity in the air made the hairs on my neck and arms
Wake up and wonder

When will it hit?

And at night when lightning lit up my childhood bedroom
And thunder rumbled me awake from sleeping
I pretended I was scared
As an excuse to go creeping
Down to the front porch
Where my parents sat watching the storm
Sitting on weathered lawn chairs they asked if I was scared
And told me I was safe from harm
As I curled into their warm protective arms

We'd watch the rain shower in sheets
And golden forks of light pierce the sky
And with a knowing I didn't yet know how to say in words
I knew the storm would pass

And in the mornings that followed these stormy nights
We'd hear on the news of sites
Where the storm had torn through trees and damaged homes
And we thanked our lucky stars that the storm had left us alone
I'd walk to school through the cool damp air and think

> *The rain has washed all the cars and sidewalks clean*
> *And cranked up the colour of the grass*
> *To make it even more green*

I wanted to bottle up the fresh fragrant scent in the air
To carry with me everywhere

When you're a kid you learn how to see them coming
And what to expect and how to prepare
But then you grow up and discover that some storms
Kinda come out of nowhere

His storm had a kind of calm before
And had I tried hard to ignore
The dark clouds that had drifted up
From our troubled horizon

I'd had glimpses of his capacity to be mean
But I could never have foreseen
How hard his storm would hit
When I finally said

> *I'm done*
> *That's it*

And the sky opened up

And instead of rain
He pelted me with punishment fuelled by his own pain
Claps of thunder were replaced with acts of slander
Flashes of lightning illuminated the frightening
Lengths to which he'd go
Seeking a vengeance that made sense only to him

His raging winds ripped through
The straw house we'd tried to build
And filled with a grief that seemed almost beyond belief
I sought shelter on shoulders so strong
And in arms so warm
And in voices that gently reminded me
This storm too shall pass

His raging winds have subsided for now
My eyes pan over the destruction left in his wake
Like a news camera trying to take
Shots of the places hardest hit

And as I sift through our relationship debris
Through the piles of pieces I used to call
Him and me
I think
Should I give this storm a name
Maybe hurricane
T W I S T E R
For the twister that picked up my life and tossed it around
And plunked me down in this new world

And so here I stand like a frightened girl
In a blue checkered dress

Clutching my dog to my chest
Looking around at the mess thinking

I'm not in Kansas anymore

And I wouldn't mind
If a scarecrow and a lion and a tin man appeared
And steered me along the yellow brick road ahead called

What happens next?

It's a trek to be sure
I've got courage
And a heart and a brain
And I know three clicks of my heels won't erase the pain
And I know that this storm that has just passed
Certainly won't be my last
And maybe I'll never know exactly how to prepare
But there is a new kind of fresh sense in the air
And I know I'll carry that with me everywhere

True Likeness

So to wrap up this journey, I want to ask what you might look like
as a map? Would you be a series of gridlines, or patches of different
colours? Would your map be like a portrait?

Have you ever had your portrait drawn?
An image of you that you could hang your hat on
So to speak and say with all honesty

> *That is a true likeness*
> *Of me*

I remember a portrait of me that was drawn
A long time ago when I was in Grade 4
Our classroom teacher Mrs Ward asked us all to partner-up
I didn't have a lot of friends and so wound up
With a moody girl called Lindsay
We were all given large sheets of blank paper
We were to lie on the sheet
While our partner traced our shape
From our head to our feet

I went first
And being the obedient
Follower of instructions that I was
I lay very still because that way
Lindsay could create the most accurate tracing
Of me

She guided the pen round my head and my ears
When she got to my shoulders
I told her to make sure she was holding the pen well
She sighed
Rolled her eyes and said

Don't tell me what to do
Just stay still will you

So I did and felt the pen as it slid
Down my arms and legs and around my shoes
I enthusiastically stood up when she was done
Keen to see this life-sized portrait
Of me

I must have made a face because Lindsay said

What's wrong
I traced you just like Mrs Ward said

Oh really
I thought
Then why is my head a funny shape
And my hair looks weird
My hands are lumpy and my legs are bumpy
My feet are two different shapes
This tracing doesn't look a thing like me
This person-y looking blob could be
Anyone

Come on

Said Lindsay

It's my turn

Okay I thought I'll do it right
And you can learn
That if you pay attention
You can draw the right dimensions

I followed each detail of Lindsay's shape
Being sure to trace perfectly around each curve
I was focused on my tracing task
But when Lindsay got up and we both stepped back
It turns out her outline looked pretty much like mine
Lumpy and odd and misshapen

Right

Said Mrs Ward

Now that you've taken a look at your shape
I want you to fill yourself in
Draw your face and your fingers
Draw your shoes and your hair
Draw yourself in any outfit you'd like to wear

I set about selecting the closest hue
For the greenish blue of my eyes
Choosing sunrise yellow to colour in my hair
Using great care to draw my lips and nose
Capturing each detail of my shoes and my clothes
Deciding that a light pink crayon hue
Would have to do to colour my skin
I was diligent about each and every detail
Not wanting to fail any part of this task

At the end of the class
Mrs Ward hung us all on the walls round the room
We looked at ourselves and some kids laughed
At ones they thought were bad
Like Conrad
Who had drawn his eyes crossed
And Scott
Who had lost his focus and made his hair way too long

And Jennifer
Who pointed to mine and said

Who is that supposed to be?

And before I could speak up and say

It's me

The bell rang and everyone scrambled to leave
I couldn't believe my portrait seemed so plain
That it didn't proclaim who I was
I had worked so hard to get it just right
All the exact colours and hues
Hadn't infused this image with any personality
This apparently wasn't a true likeness of me at all
It's funny what you recall

Now many years later
I wonder what's happened to that large sheet of paper
Probably rolled up forgotten on some storage shelf
And I think what if I drew another tracing of myself
Over four decades of topography
Would I still try to capture the details of my outer me?
Or maybe I'd draw the roadmaps within
The soul that exists inside this skin

Where would I start?
Probably somewhere around my big old heart
I'll draw a line for all the times
I travel between my heart and mind
I'll mark the points on my hands that span across
Those that I've touched and loved and lost
I'll mark the impressions left by past friends and lovers

I'll leave enough room for all of the others
Who I've not met yet
And I won't forget
To draw the cinch in my shoulders for the times that I'm keen
I'll draw the lines on my face where laughter has been
I'll mark spots on my feet for when I've run and when I've stayed
With my decisions and the choices I've made
I'll highlight my curves with sequins and glitter
To eclipse any bitter feelings that might ever arise
About thinking I'm somehow not the perfect size

I'll mark the spark in my eyes for the fact that I know
There are so many places that I've yet to go
And I'll stand back and look at my unique demography
And feel forever grateful for this awesome geography

Below is a tracing of my hand ...

... and this space is for you to trace your hand.
Call it a book version of a high-five.

How to Starve an Artist

"A beautiful exploration of nourishment – both nutritional and soulful … amazing, emotional poetry."
— *Emma Whitehall, writer & poet*

A few years ago, I was at a friend's album launch in Winnipeg, Canada. It was a really fun night full of celebration and great music. However, in the midst of the merriment I felt troubled by the state of my own inner artist. I knew that my friend had channelled passion and hard work into her album and the result was a wonderful collection of songs. But seeing this, I felt an absence of passionate creative engagement in my own life. An image came to mind of my inner artist being an emaciated stick figure, and I realised my creative self was starving.

At the time, I was working full-time for a theatre company, teaching part-time at a local university, and felt like I was constantly battling burnout. I felt like every moment was scheduled and busy and I wasn't leaving any space for creative play and discovery.

I would love to say that this moment of epiphany at my friend's gig changed my life and that I instantly cast off my workaholic ways to nourish my creative self. In reality, this is something I still regularly navigate – finding some kind of balance between being super scheduled and making time to cultivate creative ideas.

I've had many conversations with artist friends and colleagues about this. 'I'd love to work on [*insert arts project idea here*] but I just don't have time.' Sound familiar?

I realised I wanted to develop a show that explored this idea. I also thought it would be interesting to include participatory elements that I hoped might spark reflection for audiences on their own creative nourishment. For this to work, audience members would need a few objects, so I decided to assemble 'Starving Artist Kits' and hand these out to people as they arrived for the show – as illustrated on the following page. I have included notes at the start of each poem in this section to give you a sense of how these participatory elements work in performance.

And speaking of participation, I wanted to take this even further. I love to share food with people. Anyone who knows me knows that hosting dinner parties is one of my all-time favourite things to do. So if I was going to make a show all about creative nourishment, I thought why not actually make and serve food during the show as well?

My initial idea was to cook a pot of soup whilst I performed. Wouldn't that be amazing, I thought. The sounds and smells of cooking, the taste of the soup, a true multi-sensory spoken word experience. My first run of the show was to be at the 2016 PBH Free Fringe in Edinburgh and, well, let's just say that the idea of me cooking hot soup over the open flames of a camping stove in a small Fringe venue and serving scalding liquid to members of the public didn't exactly sit well with the PBH Spoken Word panel. So, I decided to make and serve sandwiches instead. The recipe is at the end of this section.

The show is a joy to perform and has resonated strongly with audiences. After Edinburgh I toured the show to the Winnipeg Fringe in Canada, the York International Women's Festival, poetry events in Durham, Lincoln and Wakefield and even to a friend's living room in Salford. *How To Starve An Artist* was also Runner Up Best UK Spoken Word show at the 2017 Saboteur Awards.

Maybe I'll do the soup plan one day.

How to Starve an Artist

I'd like to ask you a favour. I'd like you to think of the name of your favourite artist. Close your eyes. Bring the name of this artist to mind. They can be alive or dead, working across any art form. Picture their name in your mind's eye. On the count of three, I want you to open your eyes and shout their name out loud.

Ready? One, two three! Can you see it? Their name hanging in the air?

We have seen this before
These artists
These free thinkers
These creative innovators
These foul fucking stinkers
Who use art to show the world
All the problems that they see
These horrendous human beings
Are the scourge of our society

If we're not careful there could be
A call to arts on our hands
Artistic revolutionaries rampant through our lands

Poets
Painters
Musicians
Writers
Dancers
Actors
Designers
Blighters

Languishing and lazy these miscreants all
Have the vexing and annoying and exasperating gall
To be critically aware
To be movers
Shakers
Changers
There are very real and very present dangers
Of irreparable damage to our beloved status quo
There is simply no alternative
These artists all must go

Assassinations are quick
But immoral
So we must set about
Making long term strategies to starve these artists out
We must be resolute of purpose believing that we can
Join me as I take you through a detailed action plan
That is thorough and strategic
You'll agree it is the smartest
Step by step approach
For how to starve an artist

Start out early
Eradicate the arts from early childhood learning
Narrow their vocabulary
Prevent each child from learning
Ways they can express their creative yearning
If they have no words to articulate
Their inspired urges and aches
That should eventually dull desires to inventively create
Ban the asking of questions and stifle inquisitive minds
Keep their curiosity in a gripping restrictive bind
Give them fixed definitions of what things really mean
Dilute their aspirations and denigrate their dreams

Fortunately education policies are becoming ideal
To make the dream of an artist free world
Achievable and real

However
If you've missed these young ones
Failed to starve their inner artists out
And they have become grown up artists
Fear not there is another route

Start out slowly
To be effective take your time
And in incremental chunks
Start to take their time
Bit by bit they will hardly notice that it's missing
Until days are devoid of creative space
So begin by dismissing
Time to drift and daydream
Though they claim it's gratifying
Reproach them for being selfish
Brazenly satisfying
Idle indolent pleasures
Achieving nothing in daydreaming
Breed instead a steadfast belief
In the sanctity of being incredibly busy
Praise proactive practicality
Make mortgages and high wages
The sole sacred reality
Worthy of their pursuit
Tie them to mundane tasks
To keep wolves away from doors
Get them hooked on status updates
Fill their days with chores

Deploy daily duties and distractions
To deplete their creative reserves
Run them ragged
Burn them out
Fry and fray their nerves
Fill them with fear of failure
Cultivate their doubt
But if they admit to uncertainty
Then berate and call them out
For being weak and flaky not dedicated to their craft
Soon their artistic dreams will become things of the past

This technique is effective for artists
Whose craft is public and overt
But be aware of closeted creatives
Whose contributions are covert
Those who don't identify as artists
But have deep hidden desires
To one day create a masterpiece
Snuff out those creative fires

Start out discreetly
Scatter self-doubt seeds
Then let their self-doubt grow
Wild and unchecked like weeds
Then force them to feed
On the self-doubt crop that grows
A cornucopia of CAN'Ts
A hearty harvest of NOs
Serve up statements like

> *It's all been done before*
> *By smarter better people*
> *Whose efforts mattered more*

This should quell their cravings
Force them to realise
Their voices have no value
They shouldn't even try

And by following this action plan
Soon all lands and nations
Will be free of these creatives
Killed off by starvation

We'll have order
And obedience
And unchallenged control
Through and through
This is how our world could look
My friends it's up to you

Flow

I think we'll take a moment now to just cleanse our palates after such an extreme opening. In your kit you'll find a small plastic cup. If you take this out, I'll come around now with a jug of water and fill you up. In Virden, the Canadian town where I grew up, the drinking water was yellow. It was perfectly potable, but just, you know, yellow. When I moved to the big city of Winnipeg, I remember the water was clear and just tasted so different. And as I've travelled to places around the world, it's been fascinating to sense the subtle differences in how water tastes. Interestingly ...

There's a rumour I once heard
That every cup of water you drink
From kitchen taps in your sink
Has already passed through
Seven other bodies before you

Seven

    Only seven?

I reckon it's got to be so many more
When you think of all the beings and bodies
That have come before
Think of how long
We've been sharing this water for

It's not like some new water arrives
From an orbital website
Shipped direct overnight
Ready to be pumped in
At first light
Through my tap and into my kettle
For my tea

To flow through me
For the very first time

No
The water we've got
Is the water we've always had
Oh the stories our water could tell us
I bet it would be glad
To regale us with tales
About the way it's shaped
Our spaces and places on earth
About the countless times
It's broken for birth

I bet it's also a bit mad
Having been dammed up and jammed up
And filtered and fouled up
Forbidden to flow
Exactly where it wanted to go

I mean look
Forget the history books
These millions and billions of
Mysterious memory-filled molecules
That flow through me and all of you
Hold within them
The whole history of the world
The whole history of this big old lump of land
On which we now stand

Of course
It must have had its source
From which it first sprang forth
I've heard tell of a tale
Told by sages who swear

It all started with this one
Creative lady out there
Who found herself one day
Holding a big dry lump of land
In her hands
She looked at it and she thought

> *What am I gonna do with what I now hold?*

And she decided roll and mould
It into a ball thinking

> *I'm gonna make this a place for all*
> *Kinds of creatures and beings to grow and live*
> *I'll press my thumb here and here*
> *To give it space for lakes*
> *And I'll trace my fingers along here*
> *For fine flowing rivers*
> *And I'll give her a bit of a squeeze*
> *To make room for oceans and seas*

And by this point
That big old lump of land in her hands
Looked like a wadded-up bundle of trash
And the sight of this made her laugh
Thinking

> *What on earth have I just done?*

And she laughed so hard
That tears upon tears began to run
Down her face and on to the lump in her hands
Falling into the places
Where she'd pressed into the land

Fresh and cool her tears they pooled
And then trickled and gushed
And surged and streamed
Bringing life to this lump in blues and greens

Happy with her work
And the water that she'd made flow
She stepped back
Wished it well
And she let go

Sorrys

When I lived in Winnipeg, I belonged to Grands'n'More, this amazing local branch of the Grandmothers to Grandmothers campaign with the Stephen Lewis Foundation. Their aim was to do advocacy and fundraising on behalf of grandmothers in Sub-Saharan Africa who were raising their grandchildren because their own children had died from HIV/AIDS. Their work is incredible. My favourite fundraisers were the potluck suppers, where everyone brought a dish of food to share. Sweet mother of pearl, prairie grandmothers can cook! I'd load up my plate with bread rolls, salads, and spoonfuls of sublime dishes. I'd clean my plate and go back for seconds. I'd eat to bursting … and then I'd remember there was a dessert table, literally heaving under the weight of pies and cakes. I'd manage to squeeze a few sweet bites in.

And this kind of represents my creative process. I can fill my days so full of the things I need to do to keep bread and butter on my table, that I forget to leave room for the sweet stuff, like space for creative play. So we are starting with sweet stuff.

I'll pass around a tin of sweets. And I encourage you to take what you want. Don't be apologetic about it. We spend a lot of our time being apologetic and, the thing is …

I'm sorry
Is not a good way to start

I'm sorry
Is not a great place from which to depart
On a journey of ideas spoken and shared
And I often apologise before I've dared
I prepare the ears of those near me
With my pre-emptive apology

I'm sorry for taking up your time
I'm sorry for taking up this space
I'm sorry for assuming it's fine
I'm sorry for assuming this place

If my words actually hung
Like comic strip speech bubbles
Above my head
And if I cut out all the
I'm sorrys
That I've ever said
And stuck them together end to end
My sorry line would be so long I could send
It into outer space
My sorry pattern
Would reach Jupiter or Saturn

I'm sorry
I tend to exaggerate

I do have a great idea
I could start a sorry jar
Take up a collection
For each time this interjection
Seeps into my speech like an infection
Of apologies keeping me on my knees
In the face of whatever I face
I'll take a day and place
A pound in the jar
For each time I say I'm sorry
If I have a pound
For each time I say I'm sorry
Will the word still have value and meaning?

The word is defined as feeling
Regret
Compunction
Sympathy
And pity
But if I think about how often I say I'm sorry
I just feel shitty

Do I say I'm sorry because I'm sorry
Or am I sorry because I say I'm sorry so much
Do I use apologies as a crutch
To hobble along such
Times when I'm sorry is just easier to say
Times when I'm sorry is just an easier way
Along my path of least resistance
Instead of my insistence
On holding others to account
Do I really need to mount
Others' culpability as my responsibility
Bearing the weight of sorrys built
From carrying everyone else's guilt

I'm sorry
I tend to dramatise

And there are times
When I do apologise
And mean it
For having been at
Odds with someone else
Or times when I have really felt
Regret
Compunction
Sympathy
And pity

And so I reckon that it is pretty
Much time I paid more attention
To how my sorrys are spent
And try to reduce their use to pre-empt
And be more genuine with my intent
So that I'm sorry said
Is I'm sorry meant

Some of My Parts

Now that we've had our sweets, let's get to the savoury. I've got a tray of food I'll assemble for our sandwiches. I'll mix grated cheese with hummus and chopped olives and sun-dried tomatoes and spread that on bread rolls topped with some freshly ground black pepper. If you think it sounds strange, you wouldn't be the first. But trust me, it's tasty! I always feel like I'm on Ready, Steady, Cook *at this point! Remember that show? I loved that show! Two contestants, each with a bag of random ingredients, would be paired up with a professional chef – who would have to instantly create an amazing meal out of the random ingredients. Sometimes I feel like a bag of random ingredients. Like the things I've been given to 'cook' with don't always fit together. And I don't always like all of my ingredients. I'm working on it and I am getting better. I mean …*

I've recently made a couple of new friends
We hang out quite a lot
In fact we spend
Every single day together
And have done since I was about thirteen
When they first appeared on the scene
They've been around
And full disclosure I have found
I haven't always enjoyed their company
But over time
They have grown on me
Literally
These two lumps of flesh on my chest
At this point you may have done your best
Not to look directly at my breasts
But my guess is by now
You've taken a look
They are there

There is no denying
Though I have spent years trying

I've spent time deploring them
I have tried ignoring them
Each day I take to storing them in
Fabric and plastic
Elastic and wire
And to be honest I am tired
Of resenting that they are there
I want to be friends
Bosom buddies
It's just that sometimes they are frustrating
I don't get what's with my hating

According to the beauty rules
Made by controlling capitalist fools
Who determine I should feel
My goal is a fantasy physical ideal
My rack is pretty great
Or should I more delicately state
That they are a lovely shape
Proportionally dimensioned
So what is with my bone of contention
It's just man they get a lot of attention
Even from those with the best of intentions
Eyes dart and drift downwards
Unwittingly obsessed

Maybe those of us with breasts
Should put eyes on our chests
And nipples on our faces
To try to keep gazes
In more suitable places

So is that it
My envy and ego
That make me go

Ladies back off

Like some internal breast assault
It's not their fault

They're not some independent entity
Aiming for my identity to be

Rose
You know Rose
With the boobs

And so as I move
Towards accepting that
They are sticking around
Not going anywhere
Except over time closer to the ground
I've found
They actually need a lot of support
They are having an existential crisis
Trying to determine their purpose
On my human form
As a tiny human has not yet been born
From my womb with infant lips
To draw milk from them
To drink their fill
And maybe they never will
Function to fulfil this role
And hopefully they never will
Grow lumps within lumps that make me ill

Still I start to embrace them as much more
Than just objectified décor
They are part of me
Have meaning
As much as my hands
And head
And heart
And I'm learning that I'm greater than just
Some of my parts

The Swap

We've got the food assembly going well here. The sandwiches will be ready soon. It was Virginia Woolf who wrote, "one cannot think well, love well, sleep well if one has not dined well". This was from her seminal book 'A Room of One's Own' in which she also writes that 'a woman must have money and a room of her own if she is to write fiction.' I don't have loads of money, but I have enough. I don't write fiction, but I have a great space of my own in which I write poetry. I try to keep my home fairly minimalistic, but it's hard because of how much I love charity shops. Oh the treasures I can find. And I can't believe I'm going to tell you this but ...

Okay
So I didn't just wake up one day
And decide to say to myself

    I'm going to rip off a charity shop

I'd simply wandered in
One Saturday afternoon
On one of those rare days
When I had nothing else to do
But sift my way through
Reams and reams
Of second-hand shirts
And dresses and jeans
I found a few to try on
Two or three
Pulled the faded paisley
Curtain across the corner of the shop
That had opted to be the fitting room
The dress had two unfortunately placed swirls
The shirt didn't quite do up over the girls

Somewhat defeated I tried on the jeans
If only you had been there to see
How amazing this denim looked on me
From ass to ankle
From knee to hip
These jeans were a heavenly perfect fit
And I will admit
I let my gaze linger
At length over the figure I cut in the mirror
A bit like the narcissistic dog
But with denim and not a bone
And then out of the blue my mobile phone
Rang out sharp and shrill from my bag on the floor
I answered – the voice was my landlord

Come home straight away a pipe's burst in your flat

Shoving on my shoes
The call had snapped
Me out of my narcissistic gaze
As I scrambled to run home in a panicked daze

It wasn't until hours upon hours later
After I'd rescued my sodden belongings and papers
And mopped up the water I'd managed to stop flow
I decided to change out of my damp soggy clothes
And there clinging to my calves and thighs
Were these beautiful jeans
Still the most perfect size
And then I realised
I hadn't paid
I was a second-hand jeans thief
The guilt the grief set my soul churning

Kept me tossing and turning all that night
I needed to return the jeans and set things right
The next day was Sunday
Which meant the shop would be shut
But that gave me plenty of time
To rehearse my explanation and apology line

But by the time Monday rolled around
I found that I'd actually started to lose my nerve
And then it actually began to occur
To me that I'd not technically stolen from a charity shop
What I'd done was technically more of a swap
There was still a perfectly wearable pair of jeans
That were slightly worn and mostly clean
That I'd left on the floor as I'd rushed out in dread
The charity shop could sell those jeans instead
See it's fine
No theft
Everyone wins
Okay I admit it is a bit thin
My justification
I'd gained without offering profitisation
To an organisation
Just trying to put the world to rights
One second-hand sale at a time
But the thing is
These shops still have a bottom line
And sales targets that
They are supposed to hit
I mean we have to admit
As much as we're all hell bent
On believing every single penny spent
On the reams and reams
Of second-hand shirts and dresses and jeans

Goes directly into the pockets
Of those most in need
The thing is these shops still feed
Into a corporate growth machine

Which doesn't mean
You should take off and not pay
But who's to say that maybe one day
I don't have the means
To pay money for a second-hand pair of jeans
No distracted phone call
Rushing me out of the shop
But a genuine need for a genuine swap
And who's to say that maybe one day
We don't let money get in the way
Of making sure we all have the basics
I mean face it
How many of us can honestly admit
We absolutely need all of the shit
Piled high in our homes
If we all took a long hard look
At all the stuff that we've got
And brought together all the stuff
That we're prepared to swap
We could at least make sure
That everyone has what they need
And maybe we could even start to feed
The growth of a new compassionate
Social order machine
And hell you might find your own pair
Of fantastically fitting jeans

The sandwiches are ready! If you'd like to take out the paper napkin from your kits, I will come around and serve up. And since, as the saying goes, 'variety is the spice of life', I'm going to introduce another act to share words with you whilst I serve food. Please welcome my guest!

[At this point in the show a guest performs a short set.]

A round of applause for this brilliant artist! How fortunate we are to have such abundance in our midst.

I feel incredibly fortunate for the abundance in my life – food, friends, a lovely home. However, I'm reminded so often of how abundance is incredibly absent for so many people around us.

When I lived in Huddersfield, I was a 15-minute walk from my work. There were two routes that I could take. One route took me down a hill and under a rail bridge, where most mornings a man sat on the ground with a paper cup in front of him. At first, I passed by awkwardly, unsure if I should make eye contact or say hello. And then I decided to get over myself and make eye contact and say hello. I bought a pack of men's socks and one morning I offered him the socks, which he gratefully accepted. And from then on, I always made sure to bring something with me on my walk to work – a packet of crisps, a bit of change – to offer him.

On my other route to work I would pass by an old council building that was boarded up with a kind of malice that prevented people from even walking on the grass outside its entrance. And one morning I saw this and thought of the man under the bridge. I saw a building full of empty space and thought of this man who clearly needed a space to live. And – call it naïve or oversimplified – I thought here are two ingredients that could fit together. How have we not figured this out yet?

In your kits you'll find a biscuit wrapped in plastic. Can I suggest that you carry this with you and the next time you see someone who might be in need of some nourishment and connection, you offer it to them? Because in this time of abundance, we shouldn't have anyone in our midst who sits empty.

Of Home

He sits empty
His last square meal
A distant memory
A damp square
Of folded cardboard
Covers the cold concrete
Where he sits
It's far too long
Since his feet
Have had new shoes
Or socks
Without holes

He's cold
Alone

Invisible to the eyes
Of those who walk by
And temporarily
Voluntarily go blind

He tells himself
He doesn't mind
Digs hands deep
In his pockets
To warm from the cold
Digs deep in his soul for the will
To stay here until
He can fill
His empty paper cup
Up with enough coins
To buy something
To fill him up

He looks up and sees
A steady stream
Of steaming takeaway
Coffee cups
Carried by passers by
Who temporarily
Voluntarily ignore
What they consider
An open sore
On the town's skin
He can sense their
Fleeting thoughts of

What's wrong with him

He sits empty
Of humour and hope
Thinking how nice a joke
Would be right about now
A reason to laugh
Instead he leans back
Against the damp brick
Thoughts thick with wishes
For rest and a bed
And a place to lay his head
For a floor and walls
And a ceiling
To house feelings
Of home

It sits empty
Its last tenant
A distant memory
A damp square
Of folded cardboard
Covers each window
Each secured with bars
It's far too long
Since feet have fallen
On its floors
And voices echoed through
Its hallways and rooms
It sits quiet as a tomb

It's cold
Stone

Visible only to the eyes
Of those who pass by
And groan and frown
Muttering

What an eyesore in our town
Why don't they just
Tear it down

What it would give
To be a place to live
To be inhabited
By bodies

Instead
A gaudy but faded
For sale sign
Leans against its damp brick
Its walls thick with wishes
To be filled
With noise and laughter
For the spaces between its
Floorboards and rafters
To offer rest
And beds
And places for people
To lay their heads

For its floors
And walls
And ceilings
To house feelings
Of home

Scratch My Surface

As I mentioned, I used to live in a lovely flat in Huddersfield. I hadn't expected to live in Huddersfield. Growing up in Canada, I had never heard of Huddersfield. I moved there quite unexpectedly. I moved there when I found myself in the position of needing to leave a relationship. I later realised that the relationship I had left was classified as 'emotionally and verbally abusive'.

That was also unexpected.

So I moved, rebuilt my life, started over. I was determined to rise above what had happened and not trap myself into feeling like a victim. This approach worked for a while. But my body had other ideas.

I love food and have a large appetite. The great irony of this is that I also have a digestive disorder that can be severely triggered by stress and trauma. I fell very ill and was in hospital for a week. After my hospital stay, I realised that I was carrying some pretty damaging ingredients in me, like guilt and shame. I realised I needed to look inward, pay attention to them and deal with them, which I did and continue to do. And we all have this, ingredients that we carry within us that cause us harm.

In your kits, you'll find an index card and a pencil. These are there as an invitation to think about what you might be carrying that you'd like to release. At some point, maybe tonight, maybe tomorrow, maybe never, maybe write this down.

Seeing these ingredients outside of yourself can start to lead to healing. Because it's hard when they sit, ignored, just below the surface.

Scratch my surface
Gently
It doesn't have to hurt
I should tell you
You might get a bit of dirt
Under your nails
From the trails I've travelled

Traces of the places I've been
Can still sometimes be seen
Beneath my bravado
Bedded down in shadows
If I let you close enough to look
At past chapters in my book

I have learnings to re-read
Yearnings to unleash
Desires to unlatch
So please scratch my surface
I crave the sensation on my skin

I should tell you
I wear armour underneath
That is thin but strong
I've been wearing it so long
I worry I can't remember how to take it off

I worry that the parts of me that are still soft
And vulnerable and naïve
The parts of me that still want to believe
In the goodness behind actions
And in the truths of what people say
I worry these parts are withering away

I worry my heart is so hollowed by suspicion
That entry to it will only be on the condition
That no one really needs to care
I worry my eyes start to flash beware
Any time anyone stands too close

I should tell you
My heart plays host
To ghouls and ghosts
Of mistakes past
Of fools I've cast
In the roles of being worthy of my time
And I've thrown myself so many times
With eyes so fixed on the prize
Of simply being caught
That I've not always carefully thought
About who I chose to catch me
And I've let others scratch me
Too deep
Too fast
Too soon
Believing the ensuing
Sway and swoon
Was just love or lust or joy
Of being over the moon
Not noticing as the scratch
Widened to a wound
Becoming open and raw

And when I finally saw
The malice in these matches
I paused
Pulled away

Put patches
Across wounded psyche and skin
And donned armour underneath that is thin
But strong
And I've been wearing it for so long

I want a break
Respite
I just might take it off
Let the parts of me that are still soft
And vulnerable and naïve
Join with the parts that start to believe
I have the wisdom to choose a worthy catch
I don't have to lose myself in a match
These parts of me
Can let you scratch my surface

I should tell you
I'm sensitive
I bruise like a peach
But a gentle scratch can remind and teach
Me that what was once red and raw can fade
That with care and caresses
Wounds can be made to close
Become scars
Bear evidence of how far I've come

So scratch my surface
Gently
Remind me I'm alive
With the power to heal
And to love
And to fuckin' thrive

Times of Plenty

We can feel so starved of time. There is so much demand on our time, from our lives, our friends, our families, our commitments. From work and from social media.

It can be incredibly overwhelming.

One thing we always have available to sustain us – beyond food and water – is our breath. Let's all take a moment to take a breath together. Inhale. Exhale. And a wonderful thing that we can do with our breath is create bubbles. A very dear friend of mine suggested this to me once, that when I'm feeling starved or stretched, to grab a bottle of bubbles and just blow. Instant zen.

In your kits you'll find a pot of bubbles. Can we try this all together? Fill the space with bubbles. For this final poem, which is about our challenges with time, every time you hear the word "time", I invite you to blow bubbles into the space. It's a bit like a drinking game. Just don't drink the bubbles.

Remember the times of plenty
Remember having plenty of time

To spend days upon hours upon ages
Tracing your thoughts across pages
Time for ideas to be written and erased
Time when dozens of doodles graced
Endless notebooks
Remember taking the time
To look at each other
Discovering grace in glances
And taking chances
With actual conversation initiation

Awkwardly trying to sound suave or sweet
Before we redefined the words
Poke and tweet

Remember the times of plenty
Remember having plenty of time

To let your mind wander for a while
Pausing to smile at a memory
Remember remembering
Memories in detail
The pale pink flush
Of her cheeks when she blushed
The way he held his cup in his hands
Before Instagram
Became our default
Instead of storing memories
In our memory vault

Remember the times of plenty
Remember having plenty of time

To read a story from beginning to end
And spend time to reflect
Without need to expect
Any outcome
Just some
Moments for mulling
Time for the mind to digest and digress
Before we became obsessed
With crafting translations
About mundane daily occasions
Into quirky phrases to update our status
Letting our egos be fed by the likes returned at us

Before current generations
Developed new associations
For words like
Like and tag and troll and trend
And handle and follow and share and friend

Remember the times of plenty
Remember having plenty of time

To see the majesty and grandeur of forests
Before we became distracted
By tree after tree after tree
Remember taking time to step back and see
A bigger picture
Or even just a corner of our cosmos so vast
It contains everything present future and past
Casting contemplations
On what it all means
Before the perpetual presence
Of pocket-sized screens

Remember taking the time
To just be
Here and now
With more or less free
Reign to remember
That it doesn't matter
Our number of followers
Or our signal strength
Each day is still going to be
The exact same length
And we can spend our days
In the ways that we choose

If we remember to remember
How our time is used

So
Breathe
Just be here
We're gonna be fine
Remember we're surrounded by plenty
Remember we've got plenty of time

Starving Artist Sandwich Recipe

- Hummus
- Olives (green and/or black, chopped)
- Sun Dried tomatoes
- Sliced bread
- Grated cheese
- Chopped fresh parsley

Directions:
- Mix hummus with grated cheese, chopped olives, and chopped Sun Dried tomatoes.
- Spread over sliced bread. Sprinkle with fresh chopped parsley and black pepper.
- EAT. Take time to chew, breathe, swallow. Wash down with refreshing water.

The Empathy Experiment

"One of the most interesting, informative, amusing and poignant pieces of theatre I've seen in a long time."

— *Fringe Review*

As I write this, it is mid-April 2020 and the UK has just had its COVID-19 lockdown extended for another three weeks. These are strange and uncertain times.

This time last year I was in the midst of a research and development period to create my third spoken word show, *The Empathy Experiment*. Funding from Arts Council England enabled me to collaborate with incredible artists on this solo show. Dominic Berry, a beacon of brilliance in the Manchester poetry scene, provided wonderful dramaturgy. Kirsten Luckins, a super skilled producer and poet, took me through some invaluable performance coaching. Artist and performer Victoria Firth offered skill and care as a project mentor. Theatre designer Kate Morton shed light and shared insights on design ideas. Filmmaker Charles Leek took photos, designed my marketing images, and created a superb trailer. Transylvanian musician Eleonora Rosca used the poetry of this project as inspiration to compose and record music for the show.

This time last year I was doing residencies at the Lawrence Batley Theatre, Harrogate Theatre, and the Square Chapel Arts Centre to create the show. I was prepping performances for the Brewery Arts Centre and the Charlbury Speakeasy. I was readying myself to participate in the Greater Manchester Fringe for the first time. I was psyching myself up to do a full month-long run of the show at the PBH Free Fringe in Edinburgh in August 2019.

In April 2019 this show was my world. What a difference a year makes.

What follows is the script of the show. Part poetry, part experiment, part audience participation, this project attempts to answer questions that had been burning inside me for quite some time: are our addictions to smartphones causing a decline in empathy? If we all took one day each year to put our phones away and pay more attention to each other, could we collectively save empathy?

Broad questions with no simple answers. The very experience of creating the show (and attempting my own 24-hour no-mobile research periods) raised some complex issues for me around the fact that mobile technology actually has some pretty amazing benefits.

Spoiler alert (sort of) … *The Empathy Experiment* doesn't draw any clear conclusions. However, it has sparked a lot of conversation. I see how much the subject matter resonates with audiences. The show has received critical acclaim, won Best Spoken Word Show at the 2019 Greater Manchester Fringe Awards and was shortlisted for Best Spoken Word Show at the 2020 Saboteur Awards. I hear that the show stays with people long after they have seen it.

Nevertheless, here in the midst of the COVID-19 lockdown – with no clear end in sight – I can't quite fathom spending a day without my mobile phone. Compassion and empathy are shared through WhatsApp messages and video chats with family and friends. Solace comes via online sudoku. Much-needed hilarity is found in lockdown memes. How all of this will look on the other side of the pandemic is anybody's guess. But hopefully this call to cultivate compassion and nurture our empathy will have lasting power, and we can try to get a better handle on this technological presence in our lives.

Finally, a note about the audience participation. Details are written into the text about how the interaction works. At the end of this section I have included activities related to my research.

You will also see QR Codes at certain points in the text, which link to tracks of the recorded music that I play during live performances. I hope this will help to extend your experience of reading the text.

The paradox of needing to use your mobile phone while you read a show about giving up mobile phones to save empathy is not lost on me … #JustSaying.

For advice on how to use the QR Codes see youtube.com/watch?v= 8KHHFquutS8, or to access the music tracks without them please visit rosecondo.net/the-empathy-experiment.

The Empathy Experiment

(music plays as audience enters)
(set up props and hand out envelopes)
(speak to someone re. 'Shoe Swap' poem)

Hello! So, you might be asking yourselves a few questions.

Like, why is she so friendly?

And, what is this envelope for?

And, will she make me go up there?

If you're asking yourself any of these questions …

I am Canadian and being friendly is in my geographical DNA. In fact, my home province is known as 'Friendly Manitoba'.

I will explain what to do with the envelopes in a little bit, so just hang onto them for now.

I won't make you come up here – except for [INSERT NAME] – we chatted earlier didn't we? You're going to help me out in a little bit, right? Great. But the rest of you – I won't make you do anything. I won't pick on anyone or embarrass anyone. You can relax into your seats and join me on this –

(walks to performance space)

– the final part of my experiment.

(turns music off)
(LX – bring down house lights)

Welcome to The Empathy Experiment.

My name is Rose, and I have been without any mobile devices for the past twenty-three hours.

No phone. No tablet. In fact, no online access full stop.

And I have the final 54 minutes left in my experiment to tell you about how it has worked.

Twenty-three hours ago, I embarked on an experiment to see if putting away my mobile devices for one day could help me to pay more attention to the world around me. To be more aware of poverty, suffering, injustice. To raise my empathy, so it can (as Roman Krznaric says in his book *Empathy: Why It Matters and How to Get It*) be "a radical force for social transformation".

I will admit, I have been having a bit of withdrawal.

Fortunately, I have an old school, non-internet requiring device loaded with calming music to help me get through.

    (plays music briefly)

So, some of you might be thinking, who does she think she is? Some naïve, holier-than-thou vegan do-gooder hippy who wants to hug trees and save the world and who thinks she can tell me what to do?

Some of that is true. I am vegan. Sometimes. I mean, y'know. Cheese.

But I wanted to do this experiment on me first.

Then I wanted to save the world.

I wanted to do my research and share my findings and get lots of people on board and then declare an International Day of No Mobile Devices.

Why just one day? Why not once every week, or one hour per day?

Here's the thing.

I wanted this to have GLOBAL IMPACT. Something we could all do together, like Earth Day or Buy Nothing Day. Something galvanising that could unite us all across borders knowing that for this one day each year around the world everyone with a mobile device will put their phone away, pay more attention, be more empathic, be more compassionate, take positive action.

Except I don't think my experiment has worked.

Show your work. Right? That's what they say about equations and calculations and experiments.

> *(refers to an easel with charts)*
> *(puts on lab coat)*

My experiment.

I am following the experiment process I learned in my Grade 8 Science Class at River Heights Junior High School in Winnipeg, Canada.

I am going to take you through the eight steps to my experiment.

> *(new chart page)*

Step One: Observation

(brings stool centre stage and sits)

I mean ... this isn't anything new, right?

There is an increasing concern about a growing crisis of addictions to mobile devices.

I've been observing myself in this.

Case in point
Last week
I got home and it had been one heckuva day
I'd wrapped up my work and life tasks packed away
Slumber beckoned to my bed I'd soon trek
I was just gonna do one quick final check
Just for a sec
My two second scroll
Becomes a mad troll
Through headlines and clickbait
My pupils they dilate
Past bedtime it's too late
To start another YouTube binge
Just one more hit of the cringey cringe cringe

Watch the island with a hotel
With blind dates who raise hell
And judges and voters
For spouse swap promoters
And shallow fame chasers
And X-Factor placers
And come dine in my home
And never be alone
With my own thoughts

Just
Put it away / Put it away / Put it away now
Put it away / Put it away / Put it away now
Put it away / Put it away / Put it away now
Stop this scroll I want to get off

My eyes bleed and ears ooze
With leaders who accuse
That true facts are fake news
And all sides are to blame
And proclaim that with fame
Makes all women fair game
While activists insist
We bear down and resist
I'll fight back I'll dig deep
I'm tired I want sleep

Just
Put it away / Put it away / Put it away now
Put it away / Put it away / Put it away now
Put it away / Put it away / Put it away now
Stop this scroll I want to get off

My thumb stopped me in my tracks recently
I was sat on a train with my hands phone free
A pins and needles tingle made me look to see
My thumb moving on its own independently
I sat in stillness and I stared
At my thumb scrolling on its own
Stroking a phone that wasn't there

Just
Put it away / Put it away / Put it away now
Put it away / Put it away / Put it away now
Put it away / Put it away / Put it away now
Stop this scroll I want to get off

I NEED TO LOOK AWAY
I NEED TO STOP THIS SCROLL
BEFORE THINGS GET WAY OUT OF CONTROL

(new chart page)
(puts stool back under easel)

Step Two: Formulate Question

Question. How much empathy can I have when I am constantly looking at my mobile device?

Key question. What does empathy actually mean?

As part of the research I did for this experiment, I sent a survey to 100 random people across the UK and Canada asking questions about empathy and mobile use. One question asked people to define the word empathy. The overall sense was that empathy is 'the ability to understand and share the feelings of another'.

Does anyone know what language the word 'empathy' comes from?

Empathy comes from the Greek word *empatheia* meaning 'to lean into' and it is often connected with compassion, which comes from the Latin word *compati* meaning 'to suffer with'.

In her book *How to Be Human*, Ruby Wax says that "with compassion, step one is feeling the pain of another and the big step two is being motivated to relieve it".

There needs to be action. For GLOBAL IMPACT. Hence my experiment.

Right. Step Two. Formulate Question.

If I give up my phone for one day each year, will I increase my ability to understand and share the feelings of others?

Do you all have mobile phones on you?

For this last part of my experiment, would you like to join me? Would you hand over your phones?

I know it's a huge question. I've done it for the past twenty-three hours and I haven't lost my mind. Yet. Let me put on some calming music.

(turns music on)

I totally understand and share your feelings of uncertainty. I promise I will take care of them.
I will keep them safe. I won't toss them around or smash them. They'll just spend the rest of my experiment in this box.

Here. I will walk you through it.

(LX – bring up house lights)

First. You all have an envelope with a pencil inside it? Using your pencil, please write your name on the envelope.

Now. Take your phone out and turn your phone off.

Now. Place your phone into your envelope and seal it up. They are self-seal envelopes, so you don't need to lick them.

Now. Place your envelope in this box.

(collects phones)

Thank you to everyone who is joining me for this final part of my experiment!

> *(turns music off)*
> *(LX – bring down house lights)*

Okay. Phone free. Here we are. One of the questions in my survey asked people to write three words to describe how they would feel if they lost their phone. The number one word people used was ... lost.

I often go to look up something on my phone and get lost in notifications and messages and feeling the anxious need to respond or post right away. And then I look up and tons of time has passed, and I forgot what I was originally going to look up and I think, how did I get here?

I also have a terrible sense of direction. I use my phone for Google maps.

I remember, in my late twenties, travelling through Scotland in a van performing education shows in schools. Before SatNav and Google maps. My touring partner and I had a giant A to Z map to navigate with. So many times, we got lost on roads that extended beyond one map page onto another map page.

Google maps has been a game changer.

Except that now I spend so much time looking up where I am going that I forget to look up at where I am.

> *(new chart page)*

I am on...

Step Three: Research

In my research, I came across a man called Aaron Chernevak who in July 2016 married his smartphone in a chapel in Las Vegas.

Sara Konrath's empathy study at the University of Michigan found that college students were 40% less empathic than in the 1970s and 1980s.

Helen Riess says in her book, *The Empathy Effect*, that communicating mostly by screens means we miss important emotional cues and become more detached and indifferent.

(picks up Mother Goose Book)

You know who else is detached and indifferent?

You know who else misses important emotional cues?

You know who else is married to their smartphone?

(brings stool centre stage and sits)

I came across a tale in *The New Mother Goose* book of nursery rhymes that seemed to fit what I was looking at.

The tale features a character easy to recognise
This character illustrates empathy's demise
It's remarkable in fact it couldn't be clearer
How relevant it currently is it's called 'Mirror Mirror'

Mirror mirror on the wall
Who is the greatest most fantastic president of them all

You are because you are smart and strong
If anyone disagrees with you then they are wrong

Long may you continue to reign
Only you can make America great again

Good tremendous fantastic great

Wait I just have one other thing I need to say

But you've already done your reflection of the day

I know using words that you've commanded
But the thing is I'm being reprimanded

By who

It's by whom but never mind the thing is
My authority as a magical talking mirror gives
Me the power to speak to you
Which each day I'm summoned to do
Using words you've given me to say as true

Exactly that's your job so far you've been great

Actually that's the point that's up for debate
See I'm monitored by an image replication board and they detect
That my magic mirror statements are not in fact correct

What

The board says unless I start giving
Honest factual statements to you
My magical powers will be revoked

This is ridiculous
Is this some kind of joke
Giuliani
Vladimir
Who set this up

This isn't a joke and I need to speak up
I need to be honest with you and please don't scoff
Wait what are you doing can you turn your phone off

No chance you are forcing me to tweet
Hillary and the Dems
Have corrupted my magical talking mirror
Because they can't admit defeat

Surely there is some part of you that knows
That as far as being leader of the free world goes
Your lack of empathy compassion and sanity
Is doing horrible things for all of humanity

What the hell have you been looking at
For the past weeks and months and days
My successes have been really really amazing
In many many ways
I've been working so hard really hard very hard
On plans that are fantastic and hot
And by the way I'm the president not you
In case you forgot

You need to stop and look and listen

Okay then hit me with it tell me speak

No listen —

I am
I'm the best listener in the world you freak

In order to listen shutting up is required

That's it you're done you're out you're fired

You can't fire me
I've already been fired
I'm made of glass

Fine then I'll just have to kick your ass

If you break me you'll have seven years of bad luck
Which looking ahead means we're even more fucked
As a magical talking mirror it is my obligation
To speak completely truthfully no matter the situation
I believe there must be somewhere in your heart or your head
Some tiny miniscule microscopic shred
Of basic human decency or kindness or care
Or way to be accountable or loving or fair
Just take a second to consider how it might feel
To let your guard down and be genuine and real
If you show me a glimmer a glimpse of your humanity
I'll reflect back good judgement and sanity
I know it's a big ask but don't be afraid
Of backing up and backing down and letting go your charade
Aren't you tired of being so angry all the time
Mr President
Are you on your phone again

Shut up talking mirror I'm
Tweeting an order about every single mirror
Across our great land
Mirrors are killing our country people #MirrorsAreBanned

Think for a moment about what you're doing
This madness is going past the point of undoing

Too late tweet sent it's ordered it's done
No one tells me what to do not you or anyone
Tell your board to shove it you mirrors are all defeated
Hey look my post is already being hugely retweeted

Let me just say before I am banned
Without mirrors you cannot stand
And look at yourself and face your reflection
Without that there may be no protection
From how far you will go in silencing voices
And continuing your corrupt chaotic choices
So ban me break me make me face the wall
But not facing yourself and all that you've done
Might be your worst offense of all

      (puts book down)
      (puts stool back under easel)

I sometimes use my phone as a mirror. When the screen is blank or black I can check for food in my teeth. Ah. Black. Mirror. That just made sense to me.

      (turns music on)

This book reminded me of a story from my childhood. And made me think about the fact that I've always had a lot of empathy.

When I was five years old my mum read me *The Little Match Girl*.
Have you heard of it?
It's a short story written in 1845 by Danish poet and author Hans Christian Andersen
Den Lille Pige Med Svovlstikkerne
Or *The Little Match Girl*

Is about a poor young girl selling matches
On the streets of a winter's night
Barefoot and cold and too scared to go home she lights
Some of her matches to try to keep warm
Sitting in the snow these dreamlike visions form

Before her she sees
A hearth, a feast, a Christmas tree
Her late grandmother appears
Embraces her and carries her up and away
The little girl is found frozen to death
On the streets the next day

Age five hearing this as a bedtime story
I was overcome with sadness and felt so sorry
That no one noticed her suffering and had let her die
I wished I could enter the book and try
To help her or save her life
I cried myself to sleep that night

Age nine empathy drove a decision I made
At a birthday party at an indoor arcade
I discovered a five-dollar bill on the ground
I took it straight to the lost and found
Because the main thought in my mind
Was if that five dollars had been mine
I'd have been beside myself to lose it
So rather than use it for my own gain
I turned it in thinking of course it will be claimed

I'm not trying to proclaim some sort of ugly pride
I'm telling you this because I've always been the kind
Of person with abundant care compassion and friendship
My empathy muscle was toned and fit
But recently it feels like it's all started to slip

I used to send so many greeting cards to friends just because
Maybe they'd had good news or needed cheering up
I'd catch up with friends for hours over coffee or on the phone
Now I just hit like on their post to maintain our friend zone
I might post a GIF or an emoji to show I'm more invested

At best I'll send a quick message
Nothing that takes too much of a toll
On my time
And I've noticed I've started to scroll
Past posts that share really bad news
About illness or death
I don't engage or react
No condolences
No greeting card sent
No contact

(turns music off)

Show your work.

(new chart page)

Step Four: Hypothesis

I hypothesise that I will deepen my compassion and increase my empathy if I spend one day each year without my smartphone.

(new chart page with a drawing of a mobile phone)

I got my first smartphone in 2014. Before that I would declare that I wanted my internet use to be a separate, intentional activity. That going on the internet was something I would choose to sit down at my laptop to do, and not carry it with me all the time.

So, what do I use my phone for now that makes me feel like I need to have it with me all the time?

I asked in my survey about what people use their devices for. Popular responses were Google, Instagram and WhatsApp –

which, incidentally, is the only of these three words that is not yet in the dictionary. Google was added ages ago and Instagram officially became a verb in 2018.

(sticks words / images on drawing of a mobile phone)

There were some odd responses to this question.

One person wrote sharing photos of graves.

Another person put pretending to be on a call when I don't want to talk to someone.

#IveTotallyDoneThat

There were over 100 responses to my survey, and not one person listed using their device to watch porn.

#Liars

In only a quarter of the survey responses did people list using their mobile device as a phone.

Who here still has a landline?

I remember only having a landline and having to use my landline to call my voicemail for messages. And sometimes I would call my voicemail just to see if anyone had left a message. Just to see if anyone had been in touch.

Because I was hungry for connection.

In the survey I asked people to list their challenges of not having a mobile device for 24 hours. The top response? Feeling disconnected.

#DisconnectOfDisconnection

I might post that after the experiment.
I have thought of a lot of clever hashtags and posts over the past twenty-three hours.

I wonder how many posts will await me when my experiment is done?
I wonder how I will feel if when I log back in there are none?

One person who did my survey filled out the questions and then wrote the comment 'awful survey' at the end. Of my empathy survey. Lots of other people commented with questions or encouragement. Guess which comment I thought about the most.

Any guesses at what the top answer was for why people use their devices?

Facebook.

How much compassion and empathy do you think the makers of Facebook have?

Oh Facebook.

Dear Facebook
Are you wondering where I've been
What I've eaten
What I've liked
What I've loved
Who I've seen
What has made me mad
What has made me laugh
What has made me sad
What I've photographed

Do you miss me
Do you notice I've not posted recently

I bet you are bursting to tell me
What invitations are happening in the next few days
Which friends are going to events near me
Who is celebrating birthdays

I think I miss you

I remember when we first met
Back in 2007 during my MA studies
You were just starting out in the world
We became buddies
We just clicked
You helped me connect with friends old and new
I'd take a break from my books to check in with you
To see who had poked me
Or who had updated
Their relationship status
As it's complicated
Or who had written on my wall
Or had sent me a friend request
Or had thrown a sheep at me
You were the best
Way to escape for a bit
A fun distraction and it
All feels so simple
So far away
So innocent
Those early days

What happened?

I know what happened

Somewhere along the way
I decided I was okay
Giving you my everything
Which you gladly consumed
I trusted
I believed
I assumed
You had my best interests at heart

Did you start out knowing
You would become a space
That would replace face to face
That you would become a tool
Used for spreading cruel views
Where the sender was removed
From having to see
How their message would land

And I don't understand
How algorithms actually work
Or what cookies even really mean
And yet despite all that I have heard and seen
About your manipulation
About your design to be addictive
About increases in my anxiety
I still crave your dopamine fixes

Why did you have to fuck things up
In such a nasty way

And I can imagine what you'd say
   What gives Rose
   You did this on your own
   You chose your addiction to me
   On your laptop and phone

It's not my fault

Except that it is
You are not human
You were created by humans
You exist by design

And so I guess the choice
Has to be mine to take
A brain breathing break
Every now and then

Like now
So then

Though my longing for you
Grows ever stronger
I'm gonna stay signed off
Just a bit longer

(new chart page)

Step Five: Test with Experiment

That's what I'm doing. Yup. My experiment. Testing whether not having a phone in my face for one day each year can help me to increase my empathy.

(new chart page)

In my survey I asked people if they could describe how you could measure someone's empathy.

(sticks words on flipchart)

Some said no, they didn't think you could. Fair enough.

Some said observing peoples' abilities to listen and testing emotional responses.

One person said yawn.

>   (yawns)

Empathic people are more likely to reciprocate a yawn. Just seeing the word sets me off.

One person suggested using an empa-thermometer.

Except I'm not sure where or how you would insert it.

One person suggested measuring empathy using Brexit.

The most common word people used in my survey when they were defining empathy was 'shoes' ... as in being in someone else's shoes. This experiment gives me space to imagine what that is like.

>   (turns music on)
>   (places two stools centre stage)
>   (LX – house lights up)

Or maybe I don't imagine.

>   (approaches audience member)

Hello how are you
We've already had a quick chat
Remind me of your name
[INSERT NAME] yes I remember that

I know we've just met
But would it be
Okay if you came up here
To swap shoes with me

Thank you for saying yes
Can I ask you to stand
Everyone please give
[NAME] a big hand

Come up here have a seat
It's lovely to meet you
I'm incredibly grateful
For this incredibly strange thing
We are about to do

I've gotta say
It's quite nice
Not being distracted
By feeling I need to check my mobile device

Now you give me your shoes
And I'll give you mine
They might be
A bit sweaty but it's fine

Okay let's just let our feet
Settle in a short while
Don't worry I won't
Make you walk for a mile

In my shoes that would be
Hard to forgive
I just want to feel how it feels
Where your feet live

I know this might sound
Strange or absurd
But can you describe how my
Shoes feel in one word

[comment from NAME]
That was said with consideration and care
[NAME] I think your shoes are
[comment for NAME] to wear

So while we are here
Wearing each other's shoes
Can we perhaps take another
Moment to peruse

One more step
In this empathy act
Can we take ten seconds
To make eye contact

Wonderful thanks
Keep breathing keep zen
Here we go let's do this
While I count to ten

We did it we made it
Something I noticed
Was [observation to NAME]
Which I might have missed

If my phone had been near me
Diverting my attention
Okay [NAME]
I have one final question

I know this might sound
Strange or absurd
But can you describe
This experience in just one word

[comment from NAME]
That was said with thought and reflection
My word is [comment for NAME]
Which I say with affection

And gratitude
For agreeing to share
A moment with me
In each other's footwear

Let's swap back our own shoes
You take these I'll take those
Let's return to the familiar
Fit for our toes

I'm so glad you said yes
To helping me with my cause
Huge thank you to [NAME]
Please give them some applause

> *(turns music off)*
> *(LX – house lights down)*

That was great. A kind of micro experiment within my experiment.
I felt so aware just now.

#NotAPhoneDrone

Another clever hashtag.

It is weird not to post these as soon as I think of them.

Normally I put notes and ideas like this into my phone so that I don't forget.

Which reminds me of this study by a cybersecurity company called Kaspersky Lab. They explored something called Digital Amnesia, showing that we forget things because we trust our devices remember them for us – like our phone numbers. And, they say we hand over our memories to our phones.

Is this like that whole tree falling in a forest question?

If an event takes place and no one posts about it, did it actually happen?

Will we remember it?

How will I remember all of this when I switch my phone back on?

(new chart page)

Step Six: Record Data

I guess I'll remember it by the data I have recorded.

I realised it was all well and good to do this in theory. Inside, with my notes and research and lists.

(takes lab coat off)

But I needed to test my experiment out in the world.

So earlier I went out. Free of mobile devices. Ready to record all the things I would notice. Ready to be present and aware and compassionate.

And I hated it.

So there I am on a bus
And there is this little girl making a huge fuss
Wailing and whining and crying
Trying to get up from her seat
She pounds and stomps her feet
Yelling how she hates her mum
Who sits next to her in some
Kind of trance on her mobile phone
Mumbling mid scroll for her daughter to
Leave her alone
To be quiet
To stop it
To shut up
But not once
Does her mum look up
I look around at the other passengers
To catch someone's eye
Wondering if any of us should try
To intervene
But everyone on the bus is staring at screens
So I think here's my chance to up my empathy
Maybe the mum is checking her bank balance to see
If she has enough cash in her account to buy groceries
Or maybe she has an important health-related message to send
Or maybe she's at her wit's end and is having a really bad day
But honestly in that moment
All I want is for that little girl to shut the fuck up
And for her mum to look up pick her up and take her away
Happy International No Mobile Device Day

I get off a few stops early annoyed and exasperated
Frustrated with how much that experience grated on me
I'm determined to raise my compassion and empathy

I think of how many people experiencing homelessness
I see around
Sleeping rough in the centre of town
I determine that the next person I encounter
Pitched up on the pavement
Will be someone who I approach and engage with
I'll be different and kinder than everyone walking by
I'll be compassionate and caring and offer to buy
Them a cup of coffee or maybe a bit of food
And then I see him
Looking raw and coarse and crude
He is yelling at passers-by and grabbing at his dick
There is a puddle of sick next to where he sits
It's not what I imagined
It's scary and grim
But I steel my nerve and walk up to him
Hi I say
Can I buy you a sandwich or a hot drink
And he looks up at me with a smirk and a wink
And he says

> *You want to help me*
> *Get me some cash*
> *Or take me home*
> *And let me fuck your ass*

In that moment I think
Up your empathy Rose
Who knows what is going on with his mental health
Maybe he's acting like this because he's really unwell
And no wonder
The UK's austerity has led to this mess
Leaving humans like him vulnerable and homeless
And unless citizens like me take compassionate action
Situations like this will continue to happen

But I freeze overwhelmed
And I don't know what to do
And he shouts

> *Oi bitch what's wrong with you*
> *Piss off and leave me the fuck alone*

I back away
Happy International No Mobile Device Day

Fast forward to before when I'm on my way here
To tell you about this one day a year
I want everyone around the world to give up their phone
And all I can think is that my experiment is blown
I didn't speak up or speak out
Or take any kind of radical social transformational action
All I wanted was my phone to lose myself in distraction

If I can't do it
Me
The kid who cried at *The Little Match Girl*
Ooh I'm so aware and compassionate and sanctimonious
If I can't do it

And I think of when my mum read it to me
Wiping my tears
Saying it was just a story
And I want to ask her if she remembers this at all
But the thing is I can't just
Find a landline and give her a call
I mean she's alive and well
And living in the city where I'm from
But my mum is deaf
And relies on speechreading to connect
Through Skype and Facetime and the internet

Without her phone for a day my mum would be left
Isolated
Vulnerable
And bereft
Mobile access has become essential
For her to keep in touch
And the fact that I've overlooked all of this
Makes me feel like such
A dickhead

(new chart page)

Step Seven: Draw Conclusions

I conclude that my experiment has failed.

(new chart page)

Step Eight: Communicate Results

The result?

The result.

The result is that I don't want to give this idea up.

Maybe it's not one day every year.

Who would enforce that anyway? Some kind of international mobile monitoring squad?

I guess it's up to me. Up to us.

Every now and then.
Put it away.

Make room for empathy.
Swap shoes. Swap perspectives.
Really look at who and what we see.

(checks time)

I guess I should return your phones to you.

Actually can I ask for one final thing?

(puts lab coat on)

When you get your envelope back, can you please keep your phone sealed inside for a bit longer? I'll explain why in just a moment.

(LX – house lights up)
(returns phones)

Okay. Research by psychologists at the Universities of Wurzburg and Nottingham Trent showed that participants left in a waiting room on their own with their phones on a table lasted an average of 44 seconds before they reached for their phones.

Can we try this all together? Just another 44 seconds?

[NAME] can you be my human stopwatch?

When I say go can you count to 44 in your head and let me know when you're done?

And then we're done.

Ready?

Go.

(waits while [NAME] counts)

Okay. After all this time, 44 seconds wasn't so bad.

(turns music on)

So, I'm going to pass the experiment on to you.

I'm going to leave it up to you about when you want to open the envelope and turn your phone back on.

See how long you can last.

See what you notice.

Maybe you think of your own phone experiment to start
Maybe when you're walking you notice
Your shoe squeaks like a fart

Maybe you are hungry and you want to find a snack
Maybe you smile at a stranger to see if they smile back

Maybe you count how many people near you
Are wearing the colour brown
Maybe you look up volunteering opportunities in town

Maybe like [NAME] you swap shoes with a friend
Maybe you go and play a board game from start to end

Maybe you go and buy a reusable coffee cup
Maybe you just stand still and look up

Maybe you are thinking you are desperate for a wee
Maybe you are restless and want to scream like a banshee

Maybe you need to ring your mum or text your friend
Or WhatsApp your babysitter
Maybe eventually you post on Twitter

Or Facebook or Instagram about how it's been
Taking some time away from your screen

It's hashtag The Empathy Experiment and big thanks from me
Onwards we go with compassion and empathy

The Empathy Experiment
Research Survey

1. Please list the top functions that you use your mobile device for:

2. If you lost your mobile device, what THREE words would describe how you would feel?

3. Would not using your mobile for 24hrs be a negative experience? If yes, what would your top 3 challenges be?

If no, what would your top 3 delights be?

4. How do you feel about making eye contact when you are communicating face to face?

5. In ONE sentence describe what you think empathy means?

6. Please indicate your age?

7. How would you describe your gender?

8. How would you describe your cultural heritage?

9. Do you identify as having a disability?

10. What city/town do you live in?

11. Any further comments or thoughts?

Can you describe how you measure someone's empathy?

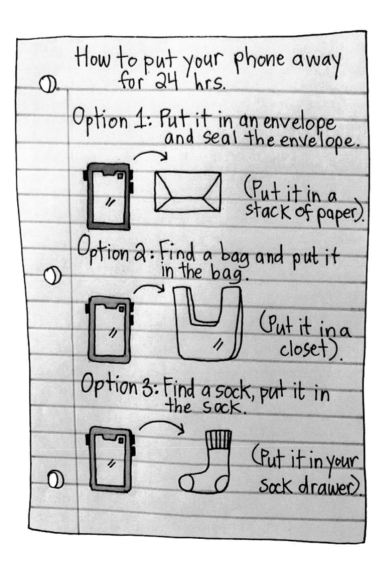

How to put your phone away for 24 hrs.

Option 1: Put it in an envelope and seal the envelope.

(Put it in a stack of paper).

Option 2: Find a bag and put it in the bag.

(Put it in a closet).

Option 3: Find a sock, put it in the sock.

(Put it in your sock drawer).

Bibliography

Konrath, Sara; O'Brien, Edward; Hsing, Courtney.
Changes in Dispositional Empathy in American College Students Over Time: A Meta-Analysis.
[Personality and Social Psychology Review 15(2) 180-198, 2011]

Krznaric, Roman.
Empathy: Why It Matters and How to Get It
[Rider Books, 2014]

Reiss, Helen.
The empathy effect: seven neuroscience-based keys for transforming the way we live, love work, and connect across differences
[Boulder: Sounds True, 2018]

Wax, Ruby.
How to Be Human: The Manual
[Penguin Life, 2018]

Acknowledgements

Enormous love and gratitude to my wonderful family:

Linda Pearce, Richard Condo, Heather Mutcheson, Graham & Tanya Condo, Sue, Abi & Sadie Lyon, Dave, Jess, Nolan & Ben Condo.

Thanks for coming to SO MANY gigs, driving me to rehearsals, helping me store props / posters / flyers, and for always being so supportive.

Thanks to Kieren for being the best companion on this wonderfully wordy adventure. Love you as much as.

Thanks to friends that are woven into the fabric of who I am:

Claire Borody, Andrea & Ray Brickwood, Shauna Briscoe, Ella Gainsborough, Ann & Rana Grant, Claire Haddon, Erin Hammond, Ciarán Hodgers, Tom Hurst, Sameena Hussain, Laura Kolisnyk, Jen McDonald, Maggie O'Keeffe, Chris Pirie, Eleonora Rosca, Brona C. Titley, Kat Vickers, Barb Voth, Adrienne Zitt.

You all mean the world to me.

Thanks to pals & poets in my wider creative community:

Matt Abbott, Su Abeysuriya, Katie Ailes, Jimmy Andrex, Lauren Ash, Hannah Batley, Pete Bearder, Dominic Berry, Jenny Berry, James Bar Bowen, Lisa Bower, Nick Broadbent, Susan Burns, Debz Butler, Genevieve Carver, Carly-Ann Clarke, Porl Cooper, Rose Cuthbertson, John Darwin, Colin Davies, Peter DeGraft-Johnson, Sarah L. Dixon, Rob Dunford, Lucy English, Louise Fazackerley, Sally Fenn, Henry Filloux-Bennet, Victoria Firth, Michelle Fitzgerald, Rosie Fleeshman, Barry Fletcher, Ali Ford, Vicky Foster, Joy France, Stu Freestone, Jac Gaile, Lorraine Gainsborough, Rosie Garland, Kevin P. Gilday, Jess Green, Sam Grudgings, Norah Hamill,

Margaret Hansard, James Hardman, Claire Hill, Michelle Hodgson, Natasha Holmes, Bob Horton, Sam Illingworth, Carol Irving, Paul Jenkins, Paul & Jayne King, Ibizo Lami, Danny Lane, Tony Lee, Charles Leek, Tyrone Lewis, Serpil & Steven Lindsay, Sharon Lowe, Kirsten Luckins, Rosa Lucy, Lisa Luxx, Carmina Masoliver, Kevin McLean, George Melling, Ben Mellor, Deb Middleton, Victoria Minton, Kate Morton, Paul & Melanie Neads, Rebecca Nouchette, Alix & David O'Hanlon-Alexandra, Karen O'Neill, Felix Owusu-Kwarteng, Danny Pandolfi, Matt Panesh, Jenni Pascoe, Dave Pitt, Winston Plowes, Big Charlie Poet, The Mayhem Poets, Steve Pottinger, Jeff & Lynda Price, Emma Purshouse, Henry Raby, Christine Renshaw, Fay Roberts, Leigh Robinson, Rebecca Roy, Martin Saxton, Tina Sederholm, Chris Simes, Dan Simpson, Chris Singleton, Alex Slater, Mick Smith, Neil Spokes, Robert Steventon, Vicky Storey, Kent Suss, Charlie Swinbourne, Rod Tame, Serin Thomasin, Viv Thompson, Kathy Trout, Scott Tyrrell, Steve Urwin, Sophia Walker, Geneviève L. Walsh, Jolene Rae Walsh, Lynn & Phil Walton, Jake Westmoreland, Simon Widdop, Dallas Wiebe, Donovan & Sara Wiebe, Jake Wild Hall, Hamish Wilson, Rebecca Winwood, Lee Wood, Brent Woods.

Apologies to anyone I may have missed. Greetings to anyone I've met since writing this list. May our paths continue to cross.

And thanks to you, dear reader, for spending time with me on these pages. Keep well. x